TRANSFORMERS

JUMBO
COLORING & ACTIVITY BOOK

Licensed By:

Look for...

TRANSFORMERS
P R I M E™

BENDON®
Publishing International, Inc.

Ashland, OH 44805
www.bendonpub.com

TF-DEC/AUT

SQUARES

TAKING TURNS, CONNECT A LINE FROM ONE
TO ANOTHER. WHOEVER MAKES THE LINE THAT
COMPLETES A BOX PUTS THEIR INITIALS INSIDE
THAT SQUARE. THE PERSON WITH THE MOST
SQUARES AT THE END OF THE GAME WINS!

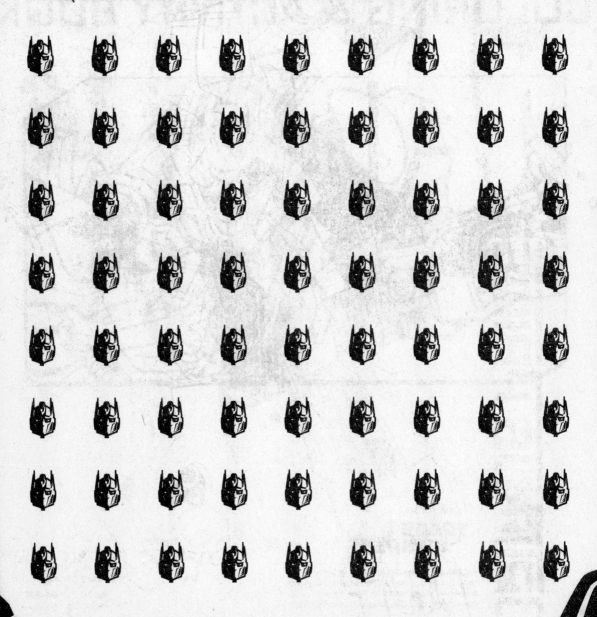

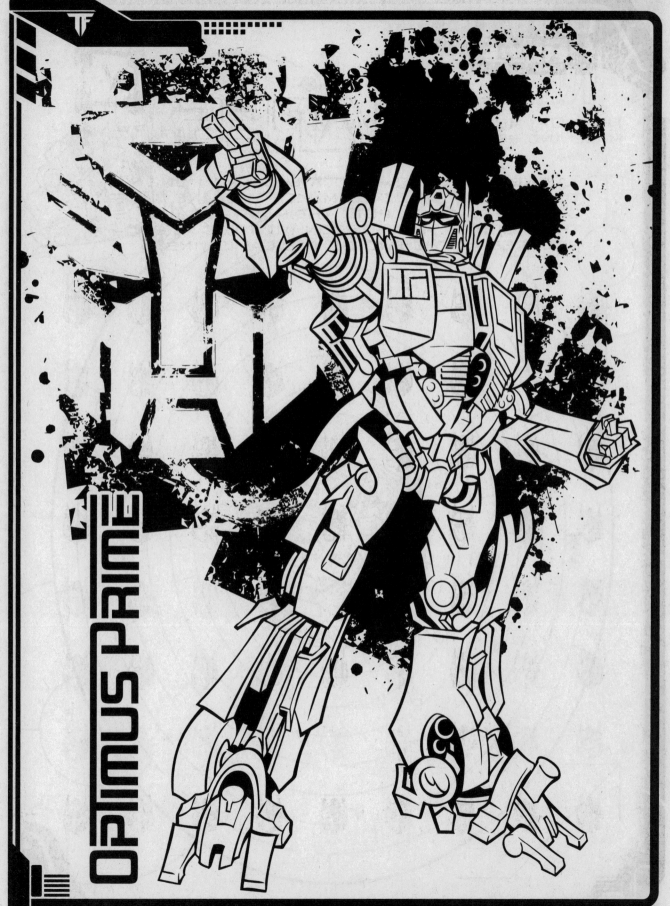

OPTIMUS PRIME

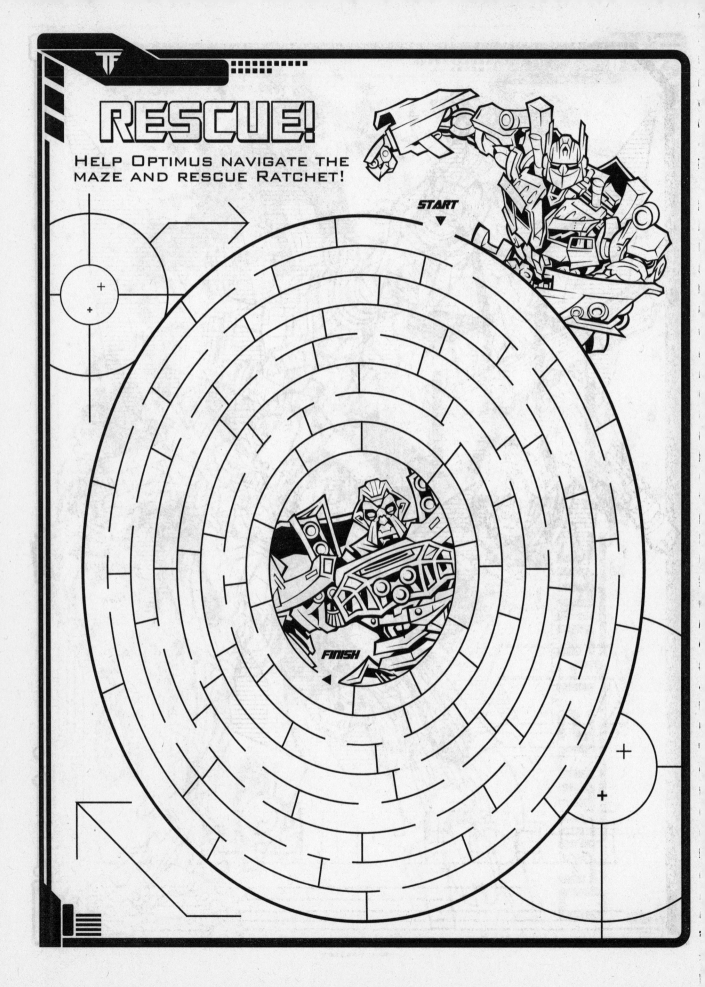

DECEPTICONS

TRANSFORMERS

WORD SCRAMBLE

Using the word list as a guide, unscramble each word below.

nietnSle mireP _____

getanorM _____

Oimtpsu emiPr _____

chSkvawoe _____

norledih _____

tSrarscmae _____

dMupfla _____

disSk _____

Rtahcte _____

Word List

- Sentinel Prime
- Megatron
- Optimus Prime
- Ratchet
- Skids
- Mudflap
- Shockwave
- Ironhide
- Starscream

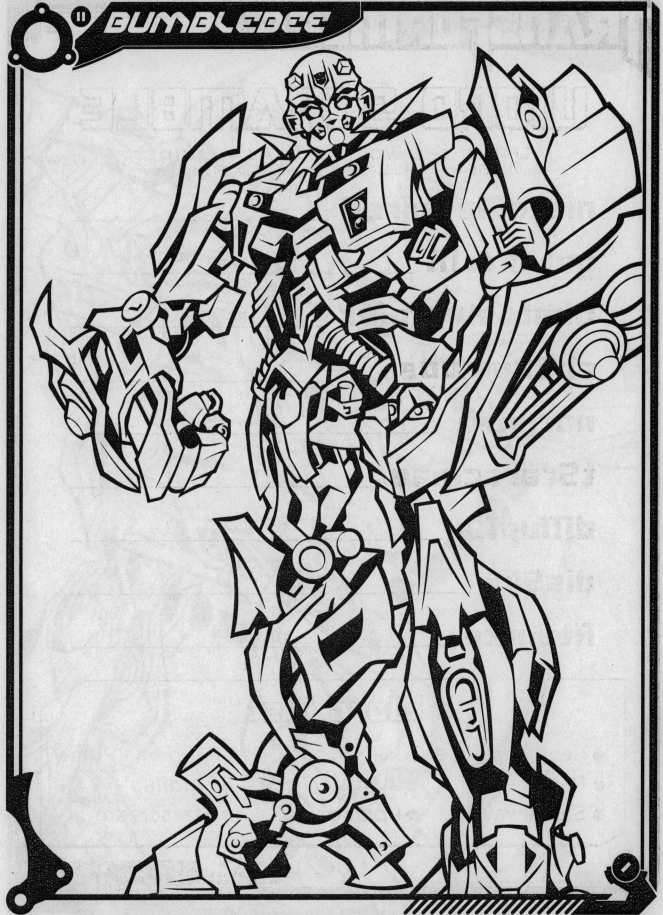

SHOCKWAVE

IMAGE SCRAMBLE

*ADULT SUPERVISION REQUIRED!

CAREFULLY CUT OUT ALL OF THE PUZZLE PIECES IN THE BOTTOM GRID. GLUE OR TAPE THE PIECES TO THE SQUARE WITH THE MATCHING LETTER OR NUMBER ON THE TOP GRID. (*VARIATION: DRAW THE PIECES IN THE TOP GRID INSTEAD OF CUTTING AND PASTING THEM.)

A	B	C	D	E	F	G
H	I	J	K	L	M	N
1	2	3	4	5	6	7
8	9	10	11	12	13	14

IRONHIDE

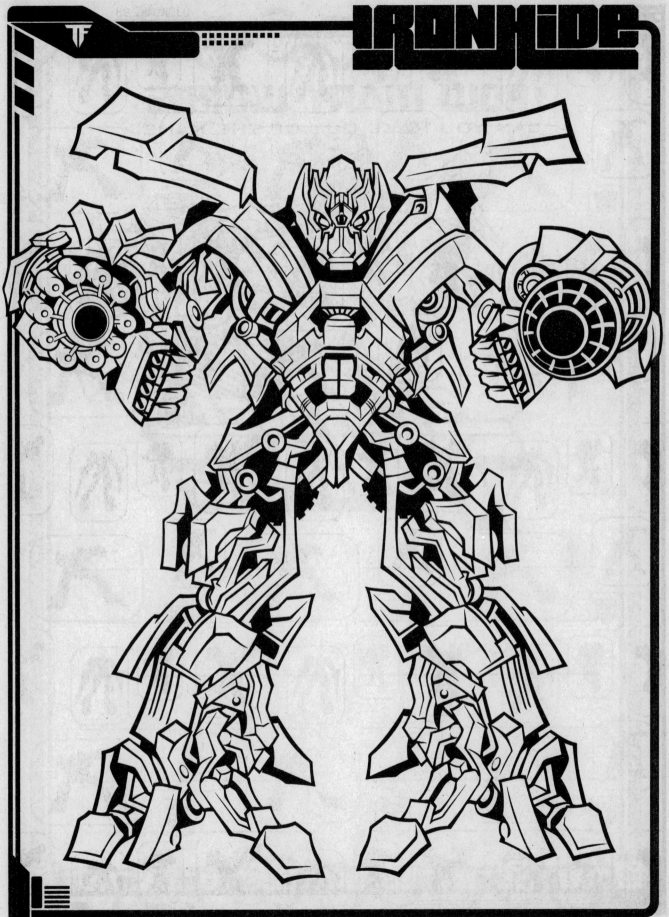

HOW MANY WORDS

CAN YOU MAKE OUT OF THE NAME:

SENTINEL PRIME

_____ _____

_____ _____

_____ _____

_____ _____

_____ _____

_____ _____

SENTINEL
PRIME

WHICH is DIFFERENT?

ONE AUTOBOT BELOW IS AN IMPOSTER. CAN YOU FIND THE ONE THAT IS DIFFERENT?

1.

2.

3.

4.

Follow the Path

USING THE LETTERS FROM THE NAME

RATCHET

FOLLOW THE CORRECT PATH TO FIND YOUR WAY THROUGH THE MAZE!

START

C	F	R	I	L	S	Q	T
N	A	A	H	E	B	Z	W
Q	T	T	C	H	E	W	A
S	P	M	J	G	T	D	C
V	H	C	T	A	R	W	Z
X	E	U	R	N	K	H	E
A	T	R	D	J	K	G	N
D	P	A	T	C	H	E	T

FINISH

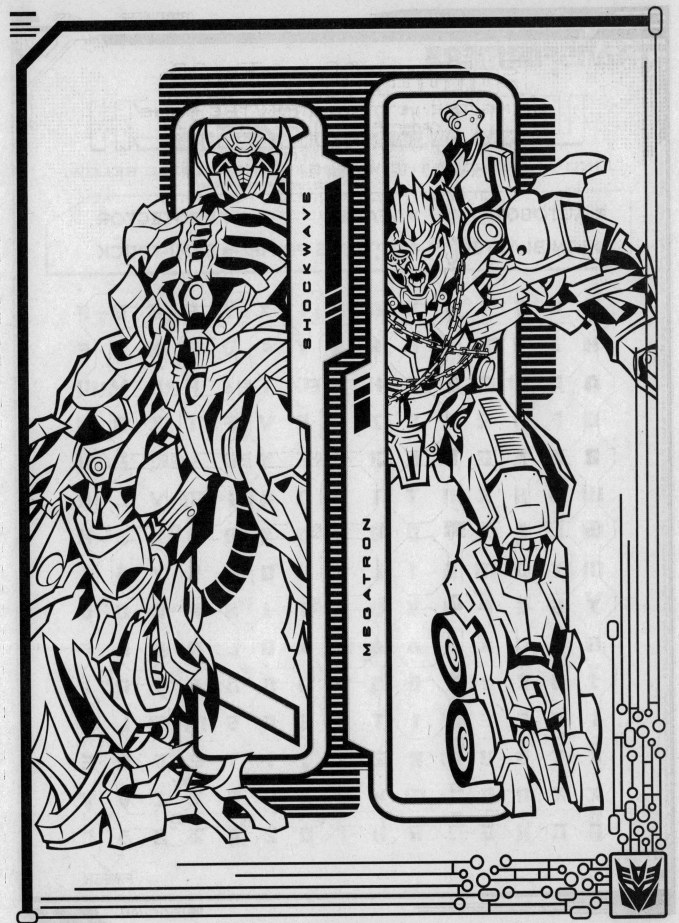

SHOCKWAVE

MEGATRON

TRANSFORMERS

WORD SEARCH

FIND AND CIRCLE THE WORDS IN THE PUZZLE BELOW.

- ⬡ **AUTOBOT**
- ⬡ **LEADER**
- ⬡ **PROTECTOR**
- ⬡ **ION BLASTER**
- ⬡ **OPTIMUS PRIME**
- ⬡ **SEMI-TRUCK**

```
Y Q T I I O N H I X Y R E B F
H J R K F F K X Y K O O X T F
A G W M F T H S C T J P H V U
Q F R Q Z S Z U C V F T T O B
Z X A Q P E R E F X O I E O H
W O H X N T T C O B I M V L N
W L C Z I O B U O X O U X E H
M Y O M R J C T H Q N S Y A I
X S E P O X U K J J B P K O C
G S U K R A A M K O L R G E F
J O C J V O A V N O A I T R I
I X C F W I T B B E S M M L E
K T B U M K Z X J I T E G O E
X K R B I M V O X C E Y Z V V
O O H G J R H I O Z R Z O A N
```

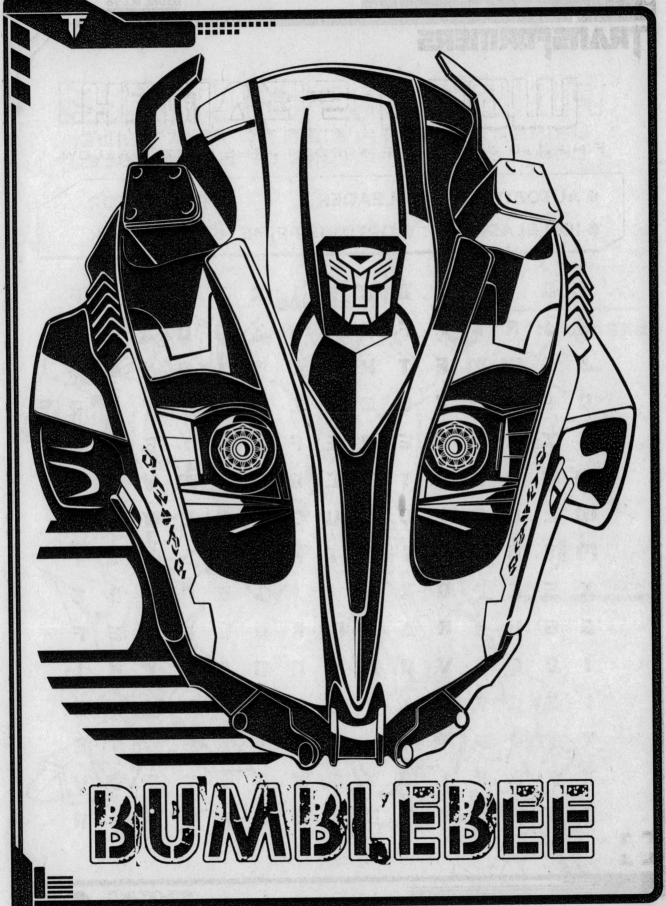

BUMBLEBEE

TRANSFORMERS

FINISH the PICTURE!

USING THE EXAMPLE BELOW AS A GUIDE, COMPLETE THE PICTURE OF BUMBLEBEE.

Example:

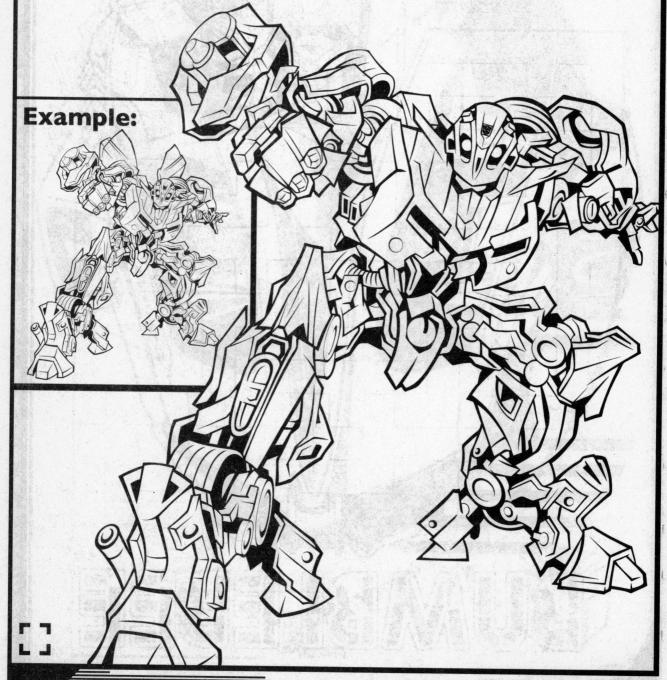

MAZE

FIND YOUR WAY
THROUGH THE MAZE!

START

FINISH

Draw

BUMBLEBEE

USING THE GRID AS A
GUIDE, DRAW THE PICTURE
IN THE BOX BELOW.

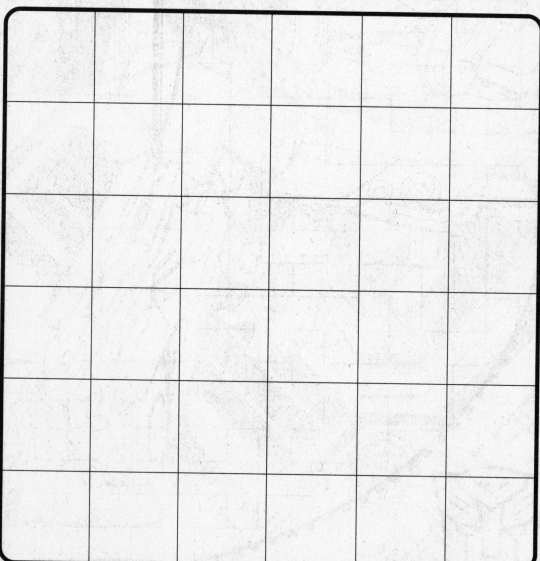

OPTIMUS PRIME

TIC-TAC-TOE

USE THESE SPACES TO CHALLENGE
YOUR FAMILY AND FRIENDS.

WHICH PIECE IS MISSING?

Only one of the puzzle pieces below will fit. Can you find the missing piece and complete the picture of Shockwave?

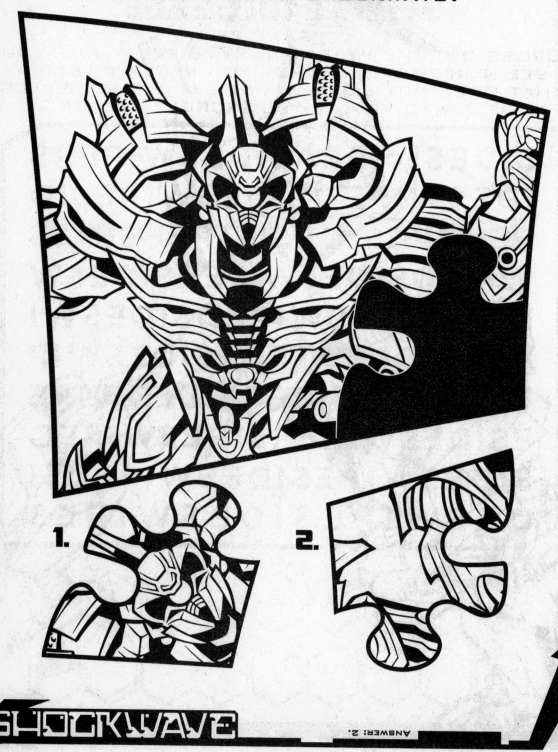

1.

2.

SHOCKWAVE

TRANSFORMERS

Sideswipe

SECRET MESSAGE

CROSS OUT THE WORD **SIDESWIPE** EVERY TIME YOU SEE IT IN THE BOX. WHEN YOU REACH A LETTER THAT DOES NOT BELONG, WRITE IT IN THE CIRCLES BELOW TO REVEAL THE SECRET MESSAGE.

```
SIDESWIPEASIDESWIPERS
IDESWIPEMSIDESWIPESID
ESWIPESIDESWIPEESIDES
WIPEDSIDESWIPEASIDESW
IPENSIDESWIPEDSIDESWI
PEDSIDESWIPEASIDESWIP
ENSIDESWIPEGSIDESWIPE
ESIDESWIPERSIDESWIPEO
SIDESWIPESIDESWIPEUSI
DESWIPESIDESWIPES
```

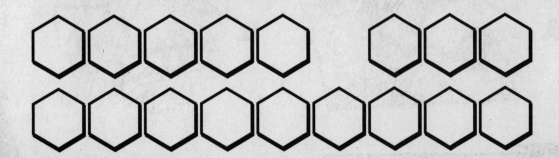

Make a Match

ONLY 2 CHARACTERS BELOW ARE EXACTLY THE SAME. CAN YOU FIND THEM?

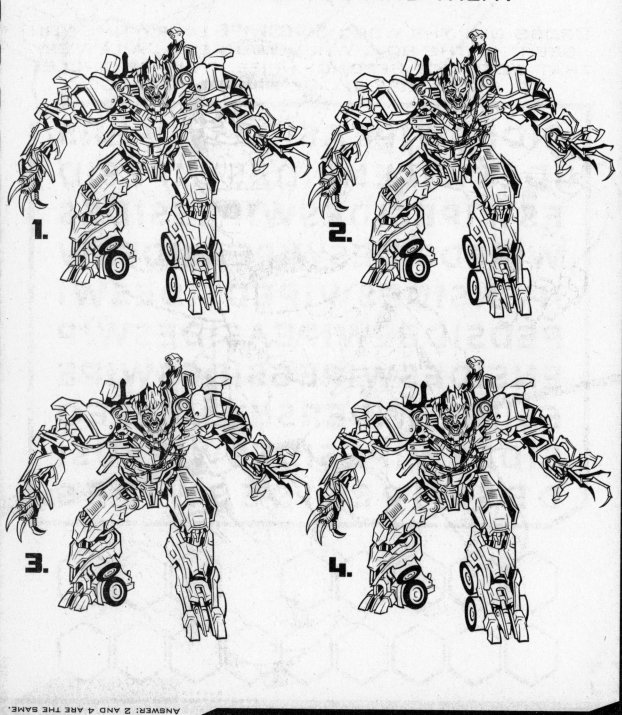

1.

2.

3.

4.

TRANSFORMERS

TRANSFORMERS

CRACK THE CODE

USING THE SECRET CODE BELOW, FILL IN THE BLANKS AND REVEAL THE HIDDEN WORDS!

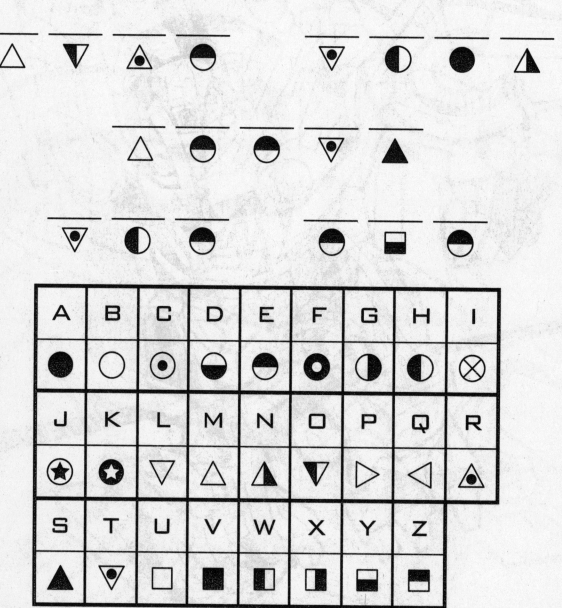

TRANSFORMERS

SIDESWIPE
TIC-TAC-TOE

USE THESE SPACES TO CHALLENGE YOUR FAMILY AND FRIENDS.

TRANSFORMERS PUZZLE

HAVE A PARENT OR CAREGIVER
CUT OUT THE PUZZLE PIECES ON
THE DOTTED LINES. MIX UP THE
PIECES AND PUT THE PICTURE
BACK TOGETHER!

■TF-DEC/AUT

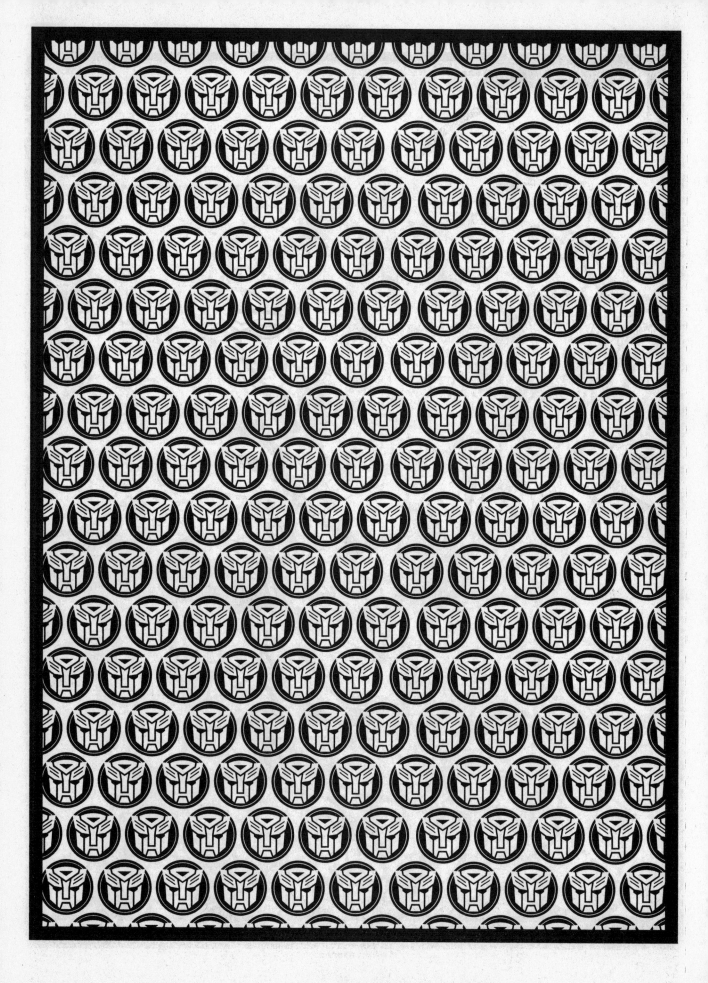

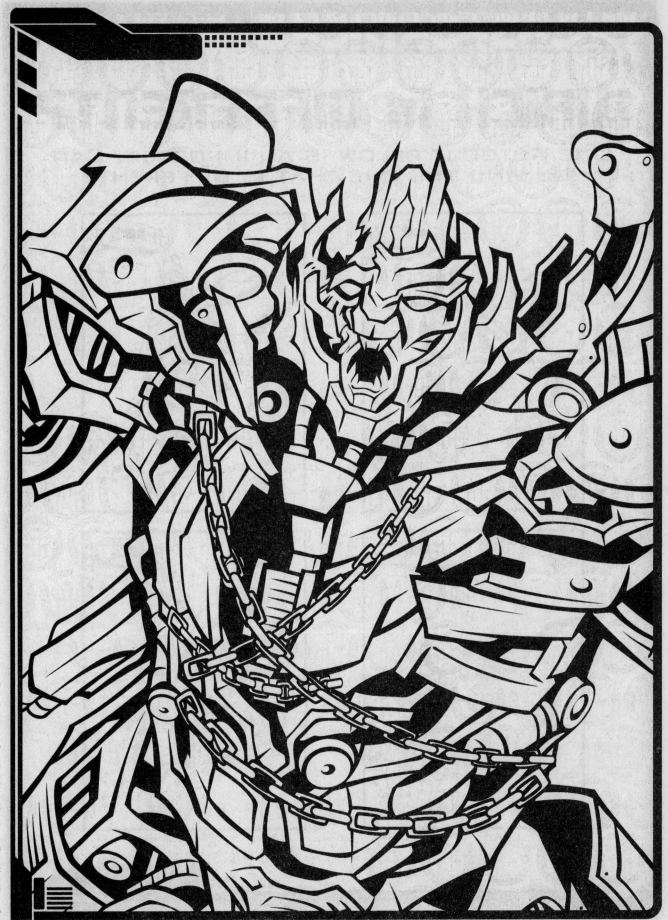

TRANSFORMERS

WHICH is DIFFERENT?

ONE AUTOBOT BELOW IS AN IMPOSTER. CAN YOU FIND THE ONE THAT IS DIFFERENT?

1.

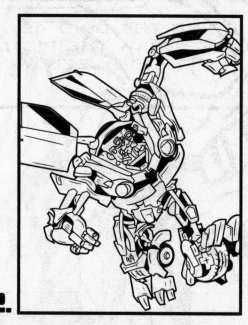

2.

3.

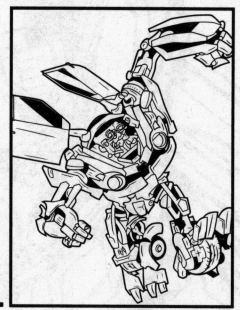

4.

TRANSFORMERS

Draw
RATCHET

USING THE GRID AS A
GUIDE, DRAW THE PICTURE
IN THE BOX BELOW.

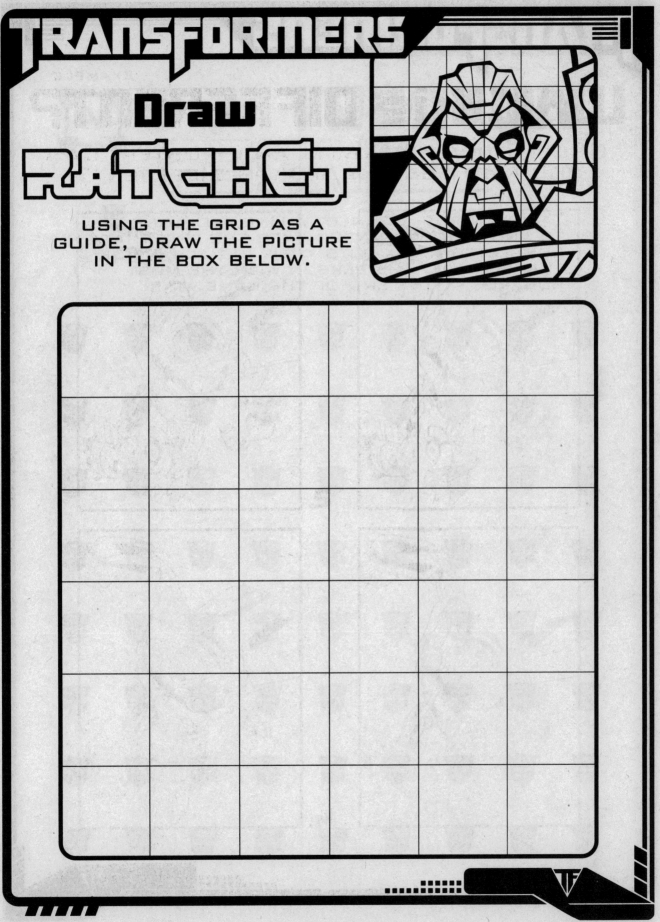

TRANSFORMERS

AUTOBOT SQUARES

TAKING TURNS, CONNECT A LINE FROM ONE
TO ANOTHER. WHOEVER MAKES THE LINE THAT
COMPLETES A BOX PUTS THEIR INITIALS INSIDE
THAT SQUARE. THE PERSON WITH THE MOST
SQUARES AT THE END OF THE GAME WINS!

TRANSFORMERS

WHICH PIECE IS MISSING?

ONLY ONE OF THE PUZZLE PIECES BELOW WILL FIT. CAN YOU FIND THE MISSING PIECE AND COMPLETE THE PICTURE OF MEGATRON?

1.

2.

MEGATRON

OPTIMUS PRIME MAZE

Optimus Prime needs your help!
Can you find your way to the center of the maze?

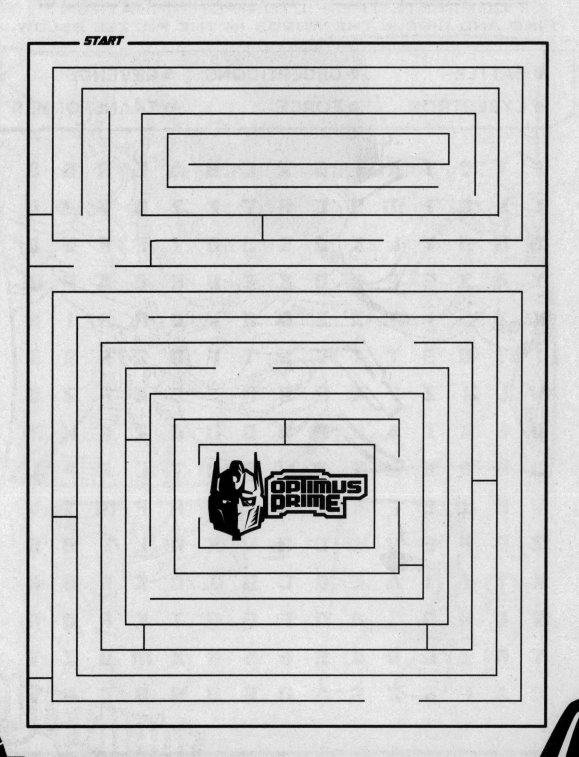

START

TRANSFORMERS

WORD SEARCH

FIND AND CIRCLE THE WORDS IN THE PUZZLE BELOW.

- BATTLE
- DECEPTICONS
- REVENGE
- CYBERTRON
- FORCE
- TRANSFORMER

```
F T C Y K I G X C B A G R G E
Y L B I M O C H Y Z Z N T A O
G B S Y L K Q S B Q J F R G Q
Y A X E E Z O K E U K O A P M
K T Q I M X E O R V O R N I R
I T O S T T C G T F O C S K K
V L I Z E K E B R C G E F Z K
D E K I A G P H O N Q Z O H M
Q O R X Q T T V N N T C R P L
V U W E F K I K C O P F M Y V
Z E F E V W C R V K N L E O B
K Y I J A E O C B W O K R E H
K E U N J A N F P P T K R Q N
Y N Z L O K S G J R X M B Z T
Q A F S Z S A N E B R B C P V
```

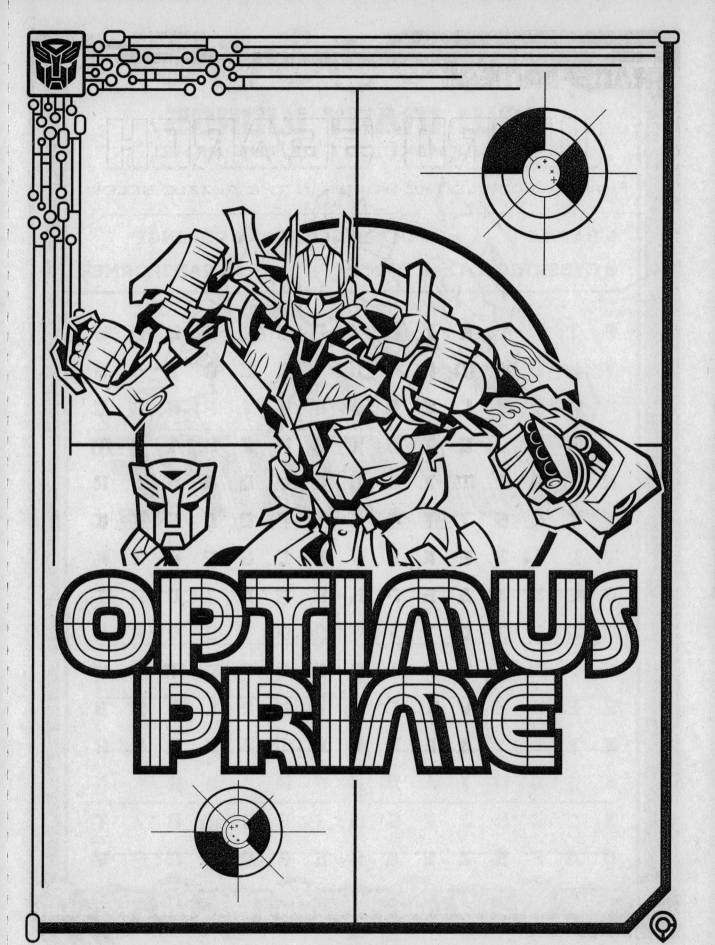

HOW MANY WORDS

CAN YOU MAKE OUT OF THE NAME:

SIDESWIPE

_____   _____

_____   _____

_____   _____

_____   _____

_____   _____

TRANSFORMERS

FINISH the PICTURE!

USING THE EXAMPLE BELOW AS A GUIDE, COMPLETE THE PICTURE OF SIDESWIPE.

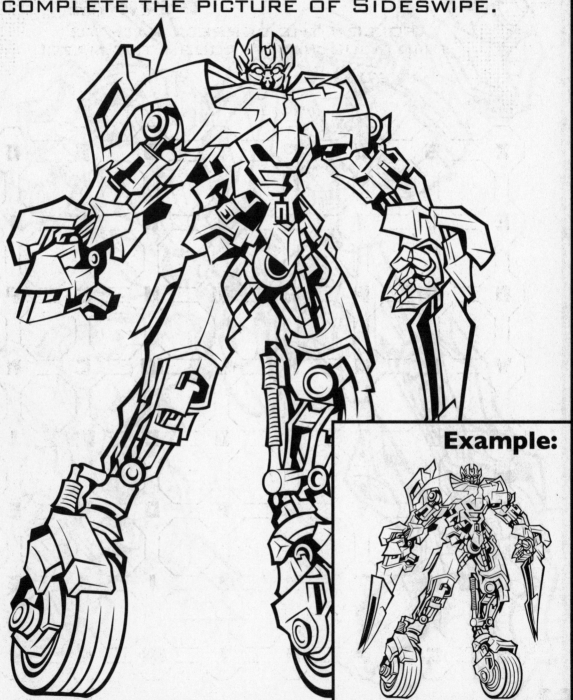

Example:

Follow the Path

USING THE LETTERS FROM THE NAME

OPTIMUS PRIME

FOLLOW THE CORRECT PATH TO FIND YOUR WAY THROUGH THE MAZE!

START

K	S	O	P	T	O	F	D
E	L	J	R	I	R	C	I
N	G	P	G	M	U	S	P
V	R	U	H	L	W	C	R
T	B	T	P	O	E	M	I
X	M	I	W	F	D	B	E
G	U	R	G	Z	I	O	E
O	S	P	R	I	M	E	J

FINISH

Make a Match

ONLY 2 CHARACTERS BELOW ARE EXACTLY THE SAME. CAN YOU FIND THEM?

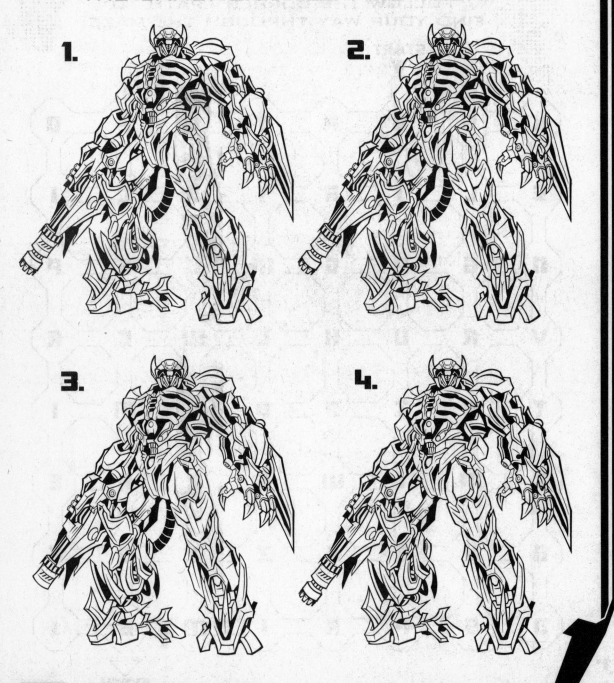

1.

2.

3.

4.

ANSWER: 1 AND 2 ARE THE SAME.

TRANSFORMERS

Draw
SIDESWIPE

USING THE GRID AS A
GUIDE, DRAW THE PICTURE
IN THE BOX BELOW.

TRANSFORMERS

CRACK THE CODE

USING THE SECRET CODE BELOW, FILL IN THE BLANKS AND REVEAL THE HIDDEN WORDS!

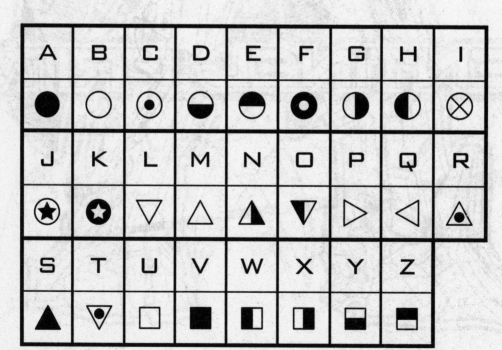

ANSWER: ASSAULT ON EARTH

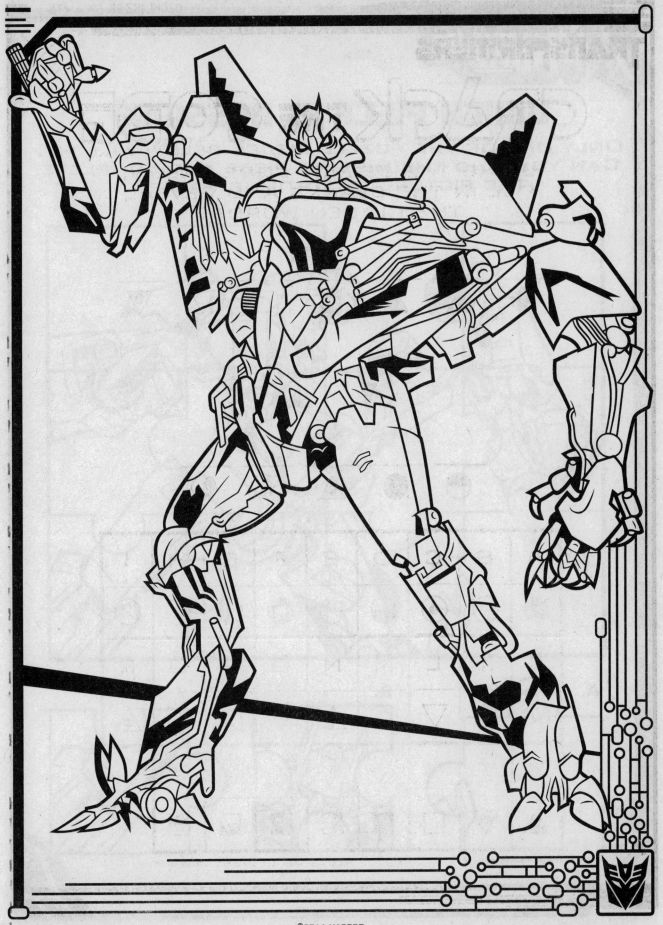

OPTIMUS PRIME...

WHICH PIECE IS MISSING?

ONLY ONE OF THE PUZZLE PIECES BELOW WILL FIT.
CAN YOU FIND THE MISSING PIECE AND COMPLETE
THE PICTURE OF OPTIMUS PRIME?

A.

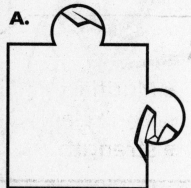

B.

C.

TRANSFORMERS

WORD SCRAMBLE

Using the word list as a guide, unscramble each word below.

pciaselist _____

hoSvakcew _____

uadigrna _____

Mdufpal _____

trngseht _____

anderguso _____

tRahetc _____

dsiSk _____

onrhlied _____

Word List

- Shockwave
- specialist
- Ratchet
- guardian
- dangerous
- Skids
- Mudflap
- Ironhide
- strength

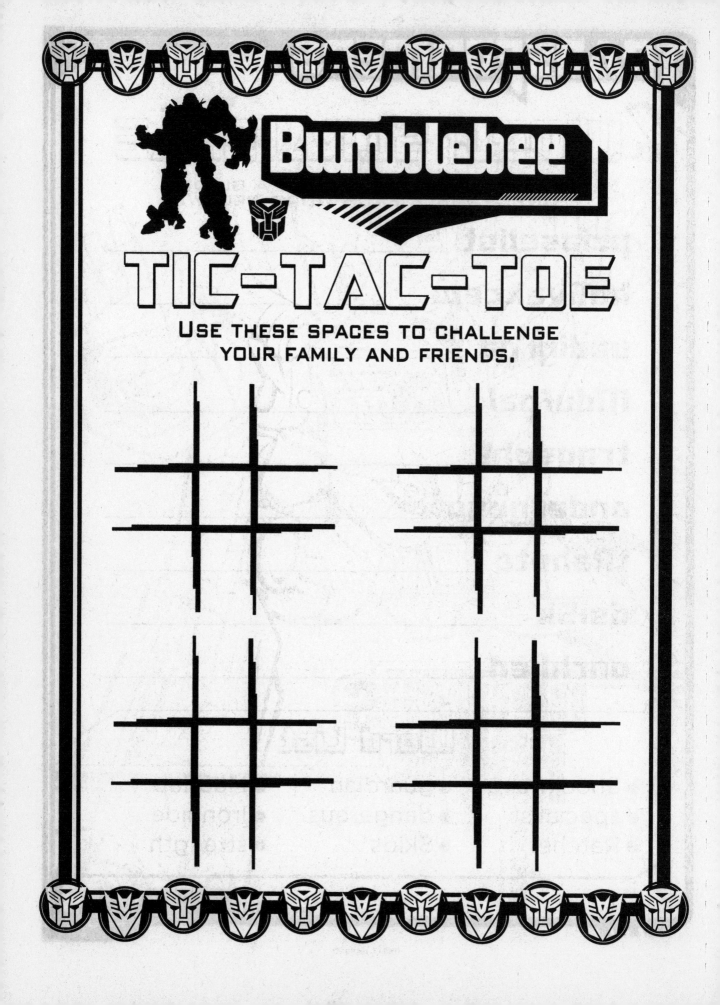

Bumblebee
TIC-TAC-TOE

USE THESE SPACES TO CHALLENGE
YOUR FAMILY AND FRIENDS.

TRANSFORMERS
Make a Match

ONLY 2 CHARACTERS BELOW ARE EXACTLY THE SAME. CAN YOU FIND THEM?

1.

2.

3.

4.

TRANSFORMERS

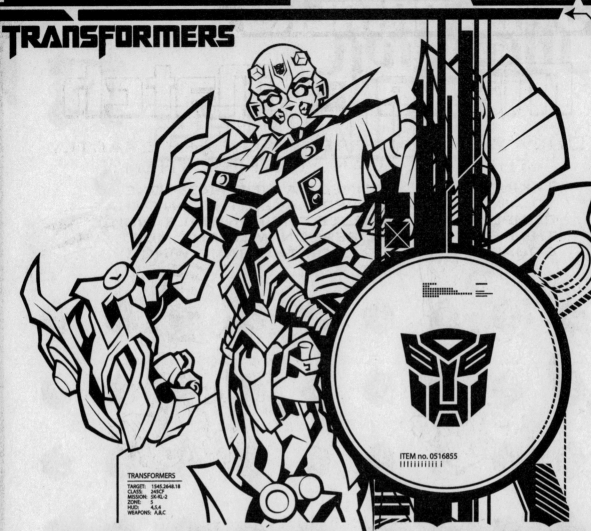

TRANSFORMERS
TARGET: 1545.2648.18
CLASS: 245CF
MISSION: 5K-KL-2
ZONE: 5
HUD: 4,5,4
WEAPONS: A,B,C

ITEM no. 0516855

BUMBLEBEE

TF-DEC/AUT

Megatron
SQUARES

TAKING TURNS, CONNECT A LINE FROM ONE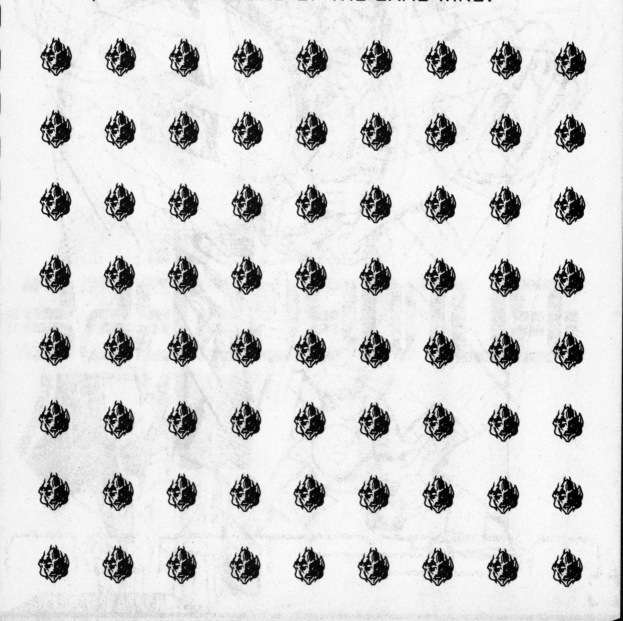
TO ANOTHER. WHOEVER MAKES THE LINE THAT
COMPLETES A BOX PUTS THEIR INITIALS INSIDE
THAT SQUARE. THE PERSON WITH THE MOST
SQUARES AT THE END OF THE GAME WINS!

TRANSFORMERS

MEGATRON

HOW MANY WORDS
CAN YOU MAKE OUT OF THE NAME:

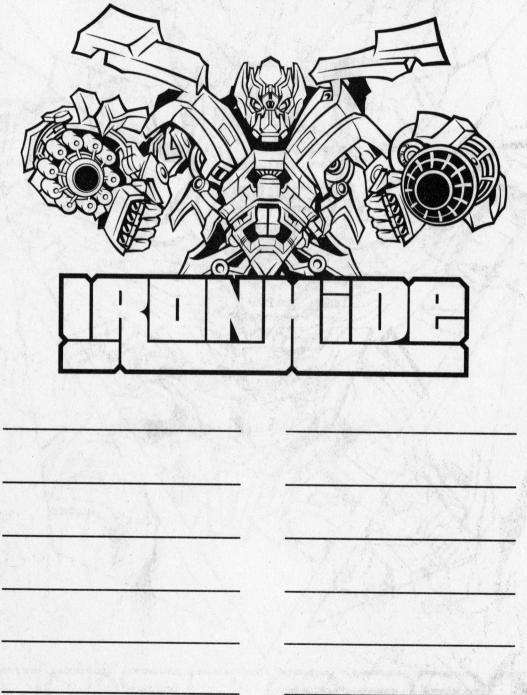

IRONHIDE

TRANSFORMERS

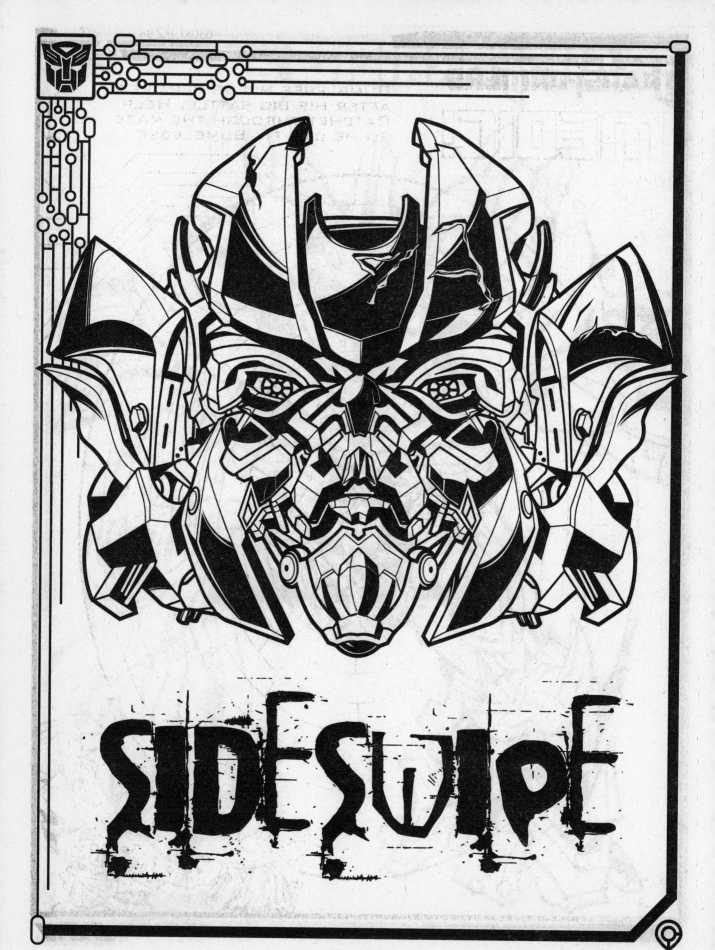

TRANSFORMERS
MEDIC!

BUMBLEBEE NEEDS REPAIRED
AFTER HIS BIG BATTLE. HELP
RATCHET THROUGH THE MAZE
SO HE CAN FIX BUMBLEBEE.

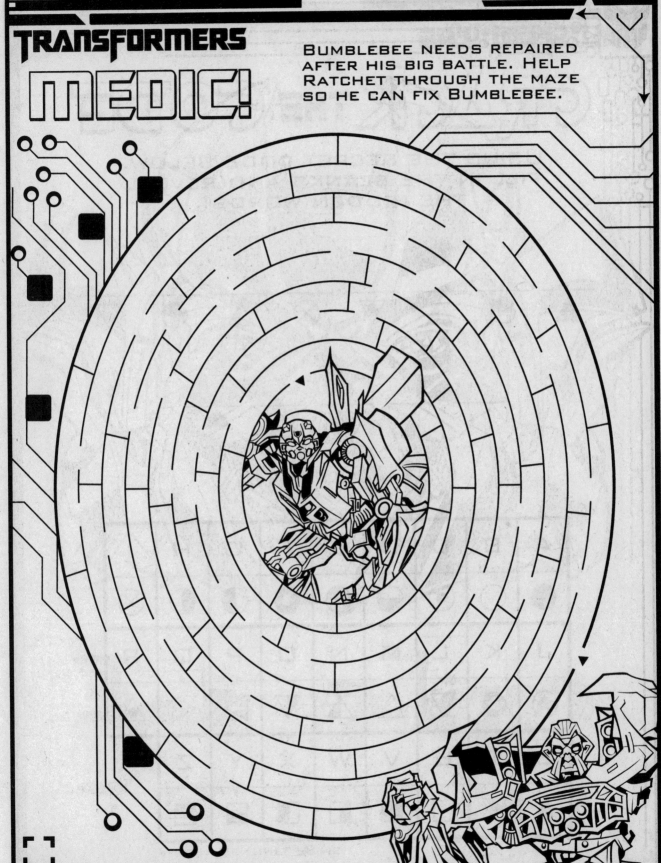

TRANSFORMERS

CRACK THE CODE

USING THE SECRET CODE BELOW, FILL IN THE BLANKS AND REVEAL THE HIDDEN WORDS!

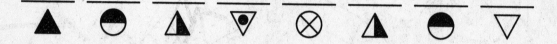

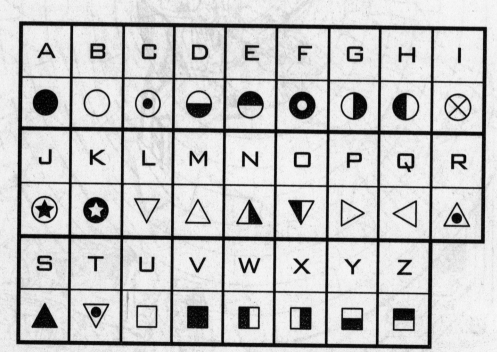

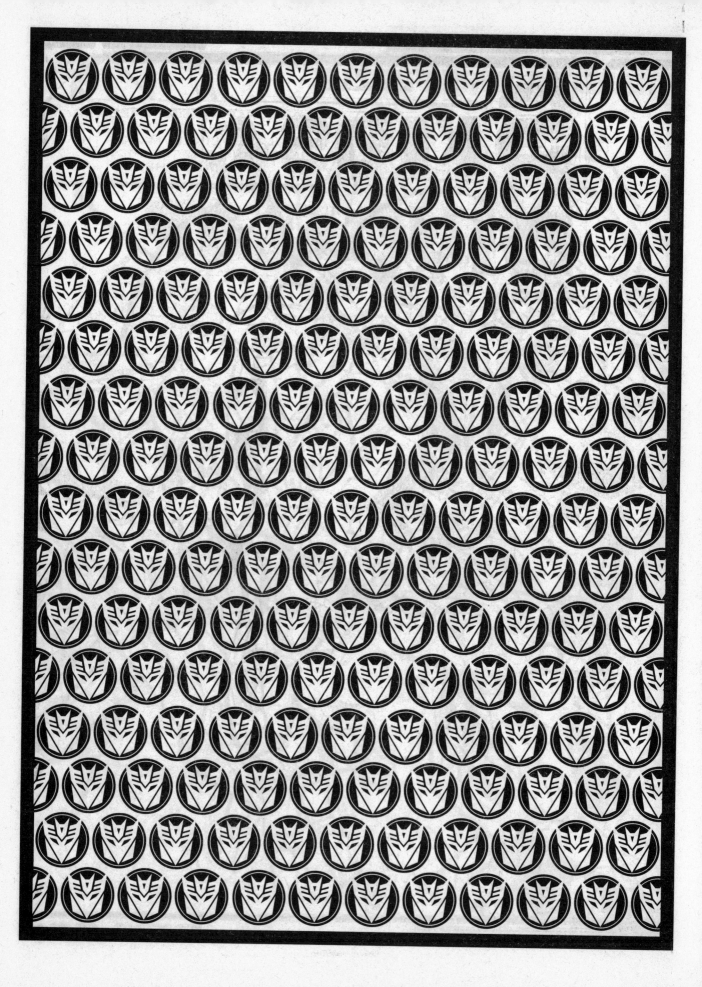

SENTINEL PRIME

Draw

USING THE GRID AS A
GUIDE, DRAW THE PICTURE
IN THE BOX BELOW.

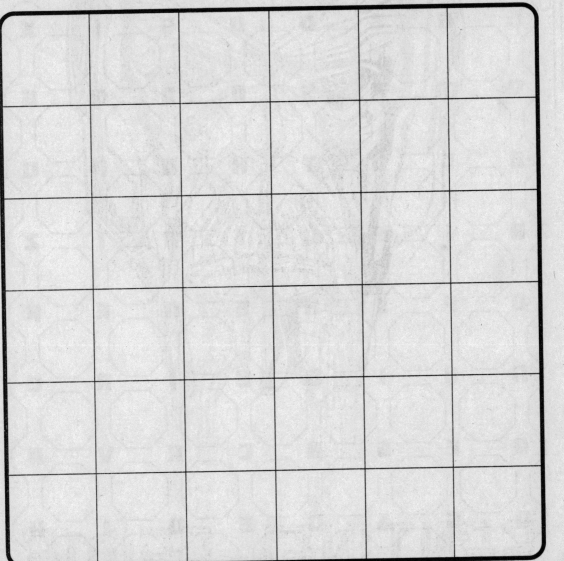

Follow the Path

USING THE LETTERS FROM THE NAME

IRONHIDE

FOLLOW THE CORRECT PATH TO FIND YOUR WAY THROUGH THE MAZE!

START

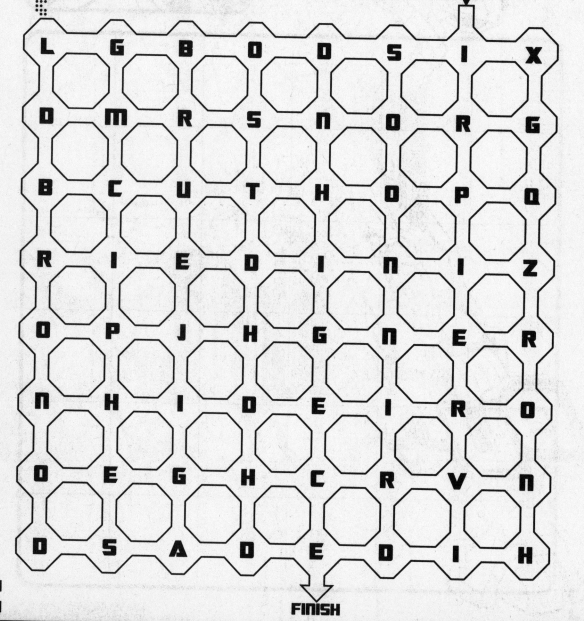

FINISH

WHICH PIECE IS MISSING?

ONLY ONE OF THE PUZZLE PIECES BELOW WILL FIT. CAN YOU FIND THE MISSING PIECE AND COMPLETE THE PICTURE OF BUMBLEBEE?

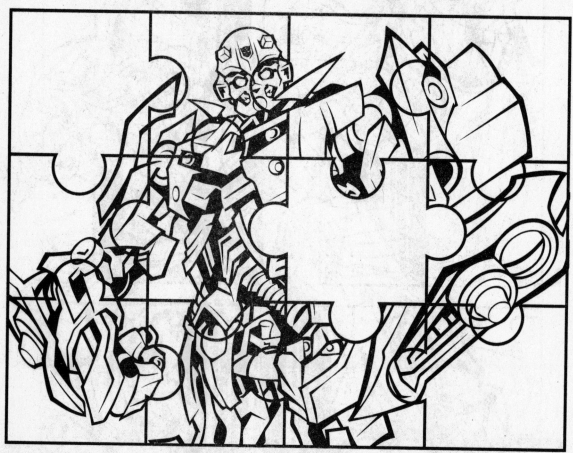

A.   **B.**   **C.**

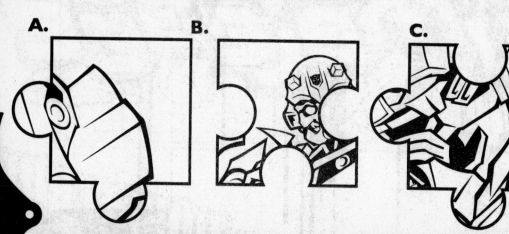

WHICH is DIFFERENT?

ONE DECEPTICON BELOW IS AN IMPOSTER.
CAN YOU FIND THE ONE THAT IS DIFFERENT?

1.

2.

3.

4.

MEGATRON

SENTINEL PRIME

TIC-TAC-TOE

USE THESE SPACES TO CHALLENGE
YOUR FAMILY AND FRIENDS.

TRANSFORMERS

FINISH the PICTURE!

USING THE EXAMPLE BELOW AS A GUIDE, COMPLETE THE PICTURE OF RATCHET.

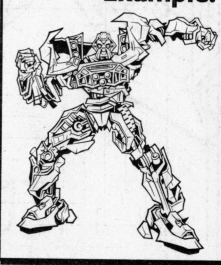

Example:

TRANSFORMERS

WHICH WAY?

WHICH WAY SHOULD SIDESWIPE
GO TO REACH SHOCKWAVE?

START

FINISH

Make a Match

ONLY 2 CHARACTERS BELOW ARE EXACTLY THE SAME. CAN YOU FIND THEM?

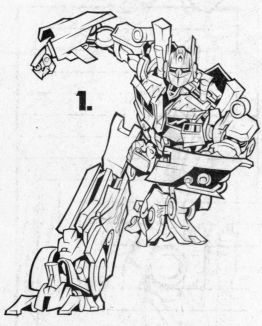
1.

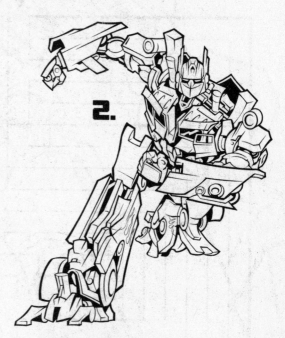
2.

3.

4.

ANSWER: 2 AND 3 ARE THE SAME.

TRANSFORMERS

WHO is WHO?

MATCH EACH TRANSFORMER
TO THEIR NAME.

A.

B.

C.

D.

BUMBLEBEE

Ratchet

IRONHIDE

STAR SCREAM

IMAGE SCRAMBLE

*ADULT SUPERVISION REQUIRED!

CAREFULLY CUT OUT ALL OF THE PUZZLE PIECES IN THE BOTTOM GRID. GLUE OR TAPE THE PIECES TO THE SQUARE WITH THE MATCHING LETTER OR NUMBER ON THE TOP GRID. (*VARIATION: DRAW THE PIECES IN THE TOP GRID INSTEAD OF CUTTING AND PASTING THEM.)

A	B	C	D	E	F	G
H	I	J	K	L	M	N
1	2	3	4	5	6	7
8	9	10	11	12	13	14

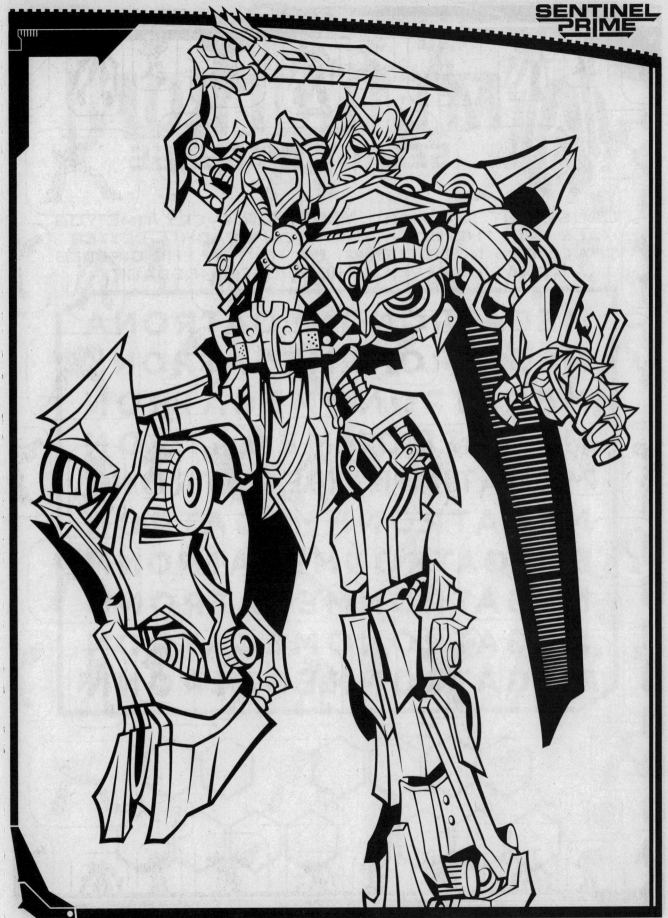

MEGATRON
SECRET MESSAGE

Cross out the word **MEGATRON** every time you see it in the box. When you reach a letter that does not belong, write it in the circles below to reveal the secret message.

MEGATRONDMEGATRONA
MEGATRONRMEGATRONK
MEGATRONOMEGATRON
MEGATRONMEGATRON
MEGATRONFMEGATRONT
MEGATRONHMEGATRON
EMEGATRONMEGATRONM
MEGATRONMEGATRONO
MEGATRONOMEGATRON
MEGATRONMEGATRONN

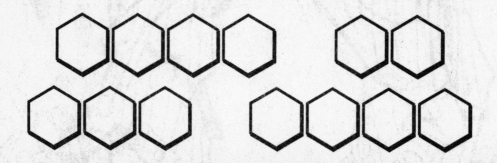

DECEPTICON SQUARES

EXAMPLE

Taking turns, connect a line from one  to another. Whoever makes the line that completes a box puts their initials inside that square. The person with the most squares at the end of the game wins!

WHICH PIECE IS MISSING?

ONLY ONE OF THE PUZZLE PIECES BELOW WILL FIT.
CAN YOU FIND THE MISSING PIECE AND COMPLETE
THE PICTURE OF OPTIMUS PRIME?

1.

2.

ANSWER: 1.

WHICH is DIFFERENT?

ONE DECEPTICON BELOW IS AN IMPOSTER. CAN YOU FIND THE ONE THAT IS DIFFERENT?

1.

2.

3.

4.

SHOCKWAVE

ANSWER: 2, SHOCKWAVE'S HEAD

Draw

USING THE GRID AS A
GUIDE, DRAW THE PICTURE
IN THE BOX BELOW.

RATCHET

TRANSFORMERS

FINISH the PICTURE!

USING THE EXAMPLE BELOW AS A GUIDE, COMPLETE THE PICTURE OF MEGATRON.

Example:

HOW MANY WORDS
CAN YOU MAKE OUT OF THE NAME:

MEGATRON

_____

_____   _____

_____   _____

_____   _____

_____   _____

_____   _____

TRANSFORMERS

CRACK THE CODE

USING THE SECRET CODE BELOW, FILL IN THE BLANKS AND REVEAL THE HIDDEN WORDS!

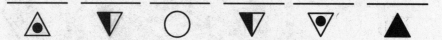

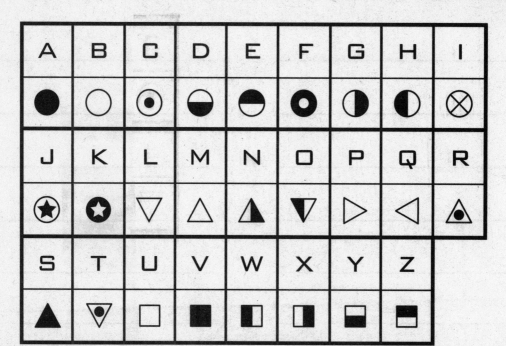

ANSWER: ROBOTS IN DISGUISE